Love More

Rediscover the Goodness and Depth of
God's Love from a Mother's Heart

Amy Artman

FREILING
PUBLISHING

Published by Freiling Publishing, a division of Freiling Agency, LLC.

P.O. Box 1264,
Warrenton, VA 20188

www.FreilingPublishing.com

ISBN 978-1-950948-35-2

Printed in the United States of America

Dedication

Dedicated to the Lord God who loves the most! I praise Him for who He is, and for His healing touch on my life and family. I pray this book glorifies Him and brings many to draw close to Him as their Savior, their Father, and their Friend.

Dedicated to my son who taught me to 'Love More' through his life and his passing from this physical world to our spiritual home with Yeshua. My heart will never be the same. The Lord our God delivers us through pain, through suffering, and through love. He is the one and only way to find peace in this crazy mixed up world. One day we will go to Brandon in heaven. Until that day comes, we will cherish our memories as a small glimpse of what is to come.

Dedicated to my family –

Dedicated to my mom, Linda. You passed from this earth so young, and yet the Lord allowed me to witness you asking Him into your life as Savior. I was only 8 years old, but I praise Him for the memories of you. One awesome day, we will be together again!

Dedicated to my parents, Butch & Shirley. You raised me to love Jesus! I am so grateful. I witnessed your daily walk with Him that began most mornings in your rocking chair with your Bible. I enjoyed homemade meals every evening for dinner. You raised me to view the church as family, and it was. I am thankful.

My husband Doran, my daughter Danielle, my son in law Harrison, my daughter in law Erika. Dedicated to my sister

Kim. She has been a tremendous support. The Lord has drawn us very close as sisters. She has supported me through the process of this book, and I'm thankful for our friendship. **Dedicated to my brothers, Chuck and Shawn.**

I know that you all hurt deeply from losing Brandon. I love you. I rely on your prayers and support. I'm grateful.

Dedicated to my grandchildren, Jace, Cash, Kai, and Ruby Jean. May the Holy Spirit fill each one of you from head to toe, as He equips you to be mighty warriors for Yeshua. My prayer for you: *"May ADONAI bless you and keep you.*
May ADONAI make His face shine on you and show you His favor.
May ADONAI lift up His face toward you and give you peace."
Numbers 6:24-26

Dedicated to Celebrate Recovery. Your CR family is a safe place for you to share your burdens, hurts and pain. It's a safe place for you to share your story. Brandon loved his time with you. CR is a place where he didn't feel judged. You all have a friendship that you share. Walls come down as you share, and that's where healing can begin. I want to encourage you to continue to LOVE MORE! Love God with all of your heart, mind and soul, and He will draw you to love all of your brothers and sisters. That love holds power to save! Philippians 4:13 says "I can do all things through Christ who strengthens me." Lord you are our Chain Breaker, and we thank you! We're celebrating RECOVERY!

Dedicated to Teen Challenge. This organization is different from most, and I think their vision statement says it all: Freeing all people from life-controlling issues through the power of Jesus Christ! Their core values, and their structure are based around Jesus. My heart will always pull for those suffering from any kind of addiction, hurt or pain. May the Lord use TC to bring glory to Him – each life changed by the power of Jesus.

I would like to thank my sweet, encouraging, ever so humble friend Darlene Newman. I am blessed by your wisdom and willingness to walk this "journey" with me. I truly am grateful for you!

Introduction

It's been almost three years since I've seen my son, Brandon. And those three years hold a deep sense of the frailty of life. Choices can't be overturned, decisions can't be changed, and the reality that there just are no do-overs with some things needs to be accepted. Hindsight isn't a pleasure that can change much for me, except to possibly help someone else who may be going through hardships in life. That is my heart for this book.

I could never dismiss even one moment of the 24 years of life that I shared with Brandon. They were years that included family vacations, holidays, worship, puppies, fast food, sports, joy and love. We were and are a family that loves deeply. We are a family that loves and is grateful when everyone is present for Sunday dinner. Brandon's absence is a silent grief we're learning to cope with.

I once told a hurting friend, that I'll never be able to say that I totally understand her feelings and journey. Not totally. I can sympathize and empathize, but I'll never be able to truly understand the details and depth of her pain. And so, I direct her to our Father. It is good for me to be alone with God for He understands me. He's been with me every moment of my life. Every joy and sorrow in my life, He has shared with me. No one knows like my Father knows. In the quietness of the morning, is where I feel His presence most. Just me and the Lord. My prayer is that you find your secret place with Him too. My hope as you read my book, is that you get a glimpse of my journey fighting for my son. But 'my journey' isn't what I hope resonates in you. I hope you sense God's strength and love that I experienced through some of the most difficult times of my life.

My personal journey is the first couple chapters of the book followed by the chapters written of basic truths found in the Word of God. I've highlighted the truths that have impacted my life. My prayer is that you journey through this book expecting God to reveal Himself to you in a very real and life changing way. Delight yourself in His word, and His Spirit will fill you with His radiant love. Soak it all up in faith, be willing to get intimate with God, and I know you will find peace.

In today's world, we often hear people use the names God and Jesus almost as common, slanderous words. It's often spoken in condemnation of something or someone. It is misused in everyday language as if there is no honor to a person or Supreme Being. And yet, as common as their names are used, there is such a lack of knowledge of their identities. We hear the names of God and Jesus in daily language, but do we speak their names as if we personally know them? Their names deserve respect, honor, and glory. God's real name was revealed to Moses as four Hebrew consonants (YHWH) or Yahweh, but in the Hebrew Bible Adonai is nearly always used to refer to God. He is Lord and yet He wants to know you and me intimately. I am using Adonai in my book for the reader to 'take in' His powerful name and His greatness. Yeshua is of both Aramaic and Hebrew origin. Yeshua is the name of Jesus. His name means 'God is Salvation'. By using both Adonai and Yeshua, I hope to take the 'commonness' away and bring an awareness that direct you to GOD. God is in His own elite category who loves us more than any of us can comprehend. My prayer is that you will say their names referencing a Holy God, a Father, a best friend, and a lover of your soul.

"My soul magnifies Adonai; and my spirit rejoices in God, my Savior." Luke 1:47

Table of Contents

It All Begins with Love

This book was birthed in my heart after the passing of my son, Brandon Neal Artman. He died from a heroin overdose on October 29, 2017. He was 24 years old. My son suffered from the disease of addiction.

Watching my son suffer from addiction, watching him unhealthy, watching him become someone he was not meant to be, and watching him suffer physically and mentally broke my heart to the degree that is indescribable. I hated that he suffered. Desperate. Deep sadness. Pain. Helplessness. If I could have 'willed' him to get better, it would have happened years ago. I wanted him healthy more than I wanted my own life. I witnessed my son's battle first hand. His journey was heart breaking for me, but I know how intensely hard it was for him living it day in and day out. I wasn't able to save him, and saving him was what I wanted more than anything in the world. I lost part of my heart when he passed.

In many ways, I feel that my life has been split in two distinct time periods: One of Brandon fighting his addiction and the other of Brandon passing. Sometimes without even being aware, I will reference the two distinct periods when talking about my journey and the Lord's faithfulness in my life. During the helplessness of the days when he was battling, when I cried out to Jesus to heal him, I was often reminded that He loves Brandon even more than I do. He walked with Brandon through his pain, and he walked with me in mine. I am so very thankful that Brandon knew Jesus as His personal Savior. For one day, we will be together again in the Kingdom of Heaven where there is no more pain, no more suffering, and no more separation. There will only be love and life! I just can't wait!

I've had people ask me what led Brandon to drugs. It's difficult to answer this question because there are different ways of looking at his life. I'll attempt to explain, trusting that you will hear my heart. Brandon was injured in a football game when he was 15 years old. This injury was the beginning of pain medications being prescribed to him by doctors. I didn't realize the destruction that can come in the form of one little pill or the degree and power of addiction. To say that I was naive' and in total trust of his doctors is grossly understated. They knew what was best for him, right? Just follow their instructions and he would heal in time, and we could go back to our wonderful lives. Right? If only this was true.

For lack of better words, I'll call his prescribed medication as an 'opening or hole' that held power to offer 'comfort and relief' while simultaneously attacking his thoughts, his brain, and destroying his whole being as my amazing son. It held power that put him in the shackles of dependency. It stole his mind. It's been said that some people can take pain medication with little side effects, but I will argue that the pills that promise to lessen physical pain can be the same pills that destroy and kill your mental peace and life. It's a deceptive exchange – even one pill can cost its victim mental anguish and a desire, a craving to want more. In my opinion, one pill can open up to an addiction.

Brandon's injury was in 2008, a time when physicians prescribed pain medication very generously. Five years of oxycontin, oxycodone, and Percocet (addicting pain medicine) was given to my son. I remember at one of Brandon's follow up visits, his doctor questioned how Brandon re-injured his wrist. It was only later that Brandon admitted trying to injure himself in order to get prescriptions of pain medicine. He was desperate. He was addicted. Did the doctors see the signs? Did we see the signs?

Maybe we all saw some warning signs, but wanted to believe that he was going to be okay and that the cycle of pain and medication was going to pass with time. He was young, and his mind was being changed in ways none of us fully understood.

The other side of the story is to be honest about Brandon, and also us as his parents. We knew he was dabbling in marijuana in high school. We knew he was drinking and being reckless. We knew that he thought he was invincible. He wasn't shy about expressing his opinion on the right to get high on marijuana. As his parents, we punished him, we set boundaries, we fought hard, but we also brushed off some of his behavior as a 'normal teenage stage'. We viewed his curiosity as a stage that he was going to outgrow. We, too, had lived a little crazy in our teens and early 20's and look at us. We survived. Right? Drugs have always changed the brain and offered a temporary euphoria, but today one single use of a given substance can change a person's life. Drugs are weapons straight from hell, designed to kill and destroy a person's life. My heart breaks to remember my foolish deception. Yes, we did drink and dabble in drugs, but how many of our friends and family members, couldn't dabble? How many people in our lives had we already witnessed the destruction from drugs and alcohol abuse? And yet we viewed his experimental curiosity as something 'normal' that he would outgrow. We just didn't take it seriously enough. There are many days that I regret my lack of insight to the Lord. My sincere prayer is that my message will serve as a warning and other parents will not take their child's curiosity of drugs and alcohol lightly. I should never have viewed his drug use as normal. It is not normal.

I remember the day that Brandon was told by a doctor in Philadelphia that he no longer would write a prescription for pain medicine. I had shared with the doctor that I was concerned that Brandon may be dependent on the pain medicine. He looked right at Brandon and said, 'If you think having pain in your wrist is hard, and you have developed an addiction to pain meds, then you have no idea the real pain ahead of you'! And with that, he walked out the door never to see Brandon again. There was no help offered. There were no resources given to us. Nothing. Just a 'so long buddy and good riddance'. I'll never forget the look on Brandon's face. Five years of being prescribed pain medication was instantly stopped. He was scared and so was I. I know that is when he went to the streets to supply his pain meds.

Brandon was married in his early 20's to Erika. They were high school sweethearts. Together they had a beautiful son, Jace. He was a husband and father while fighting his disease. He loved his family very much. As much as he fought to get better for them and for himself, the power of drugs seemed greater. He was very sick.

I'll never forget the time his addiction began to spiral out of control. Brandon received two Driving While Intoxicated in ten days. Two DWI's in the state of Pennsylvania means guaranteed jail time. Brandon was caught driving while impaired of marijuana and pain medication. The day of his sentencing in court is a heartbreaking memory for me.

My daughter Danielle and I sat in the courtroom waiting with Brandon. We sat in the very back row with his lawyer. After all day of watching sentence after sentence being given, Brandon was the last case of the day. I was saddened for the people who stood on trial that day. I know that they were there for breaking the law, and I know we need justice in place. It's the disrespect given to them by the officers and judge that was so heart breaking. At one point, the two officers were laughing and making fun of one of the defendants. It was wrong. I've been told that the courts become 'numb' to cases and that to them it's common or even comical. I'm here to say, it's not funny and no person should be mocked.

Finally, when Brandon approached the bench, the judge reviewed Brandon's history. He had 2 DWI's in one month with no history of any other charges. The judge asked Brandon some questions in regards to his drug use. He asked him in a very demeaning way how Brandon chose to use heroin. Did he snort it? Did he eat it? Did he shoot it in his arm with a needle? Brandon's head hung low. The judge then went on to laugh about a party he had attended, and how a lawyer stated that there is no connection between pain medicine and heroin. The judge was righteous and preached that until people start educating themselves on this problem, we are never going to see change in our world. Brandon was given his sentence – 30 days in jail. But before we left, the judge looked back at me and my daughter. He disrespectfully quoted statistics of the rise of women using heroin. It was a one minute pointing a finger at us warning. We were dressed nicely that day, tears were flowing all day as we sat silent waiting Brandon's sentence, and yet what made that judge treat us with such disrespect? I assume it was our association to Brandon. His disrespect was wrong. I left there with a broken heart for many reasons. It was a very hard day for all of us, knowing that every day the courts are filled with brokenness and people regarded as worthless. Society mocks their pain. These memories should push me to my knees every day to pray for these hurting in our world. I hated that Brandon was hurting. I hated seeing him broken. Please pray with me for the hurting.

We hired a 'life coach' for Brandon shortly after his sentence was over. This man was to be a confidant to Brandon. He was to be a counselor and to help bridge the communication gap and misunderstandings that happen between family members when fighting the disease of addiction. He helped us establish boundaries and accountability. He tried to orchestrate peace and understanding between us all, but lies and deception continued to be part of Brandon's illness. The counselor helped us find a facility in Florida for Brandon to enter his first rehab. I remember our conversations as my husband drove Brandon to the Philadelphia airport on New Year's Eve. Brandon was nervous and yet very hopeful. He wanted to change. He wanted to be well again. Tears flooded at the airport as we said 'goodbye'. We were all desperate for recovery. We were all desperate for peace.

The first 10 days while Brandon was in rehab meant no communication of any kind. It is normal procedure to take phones and shut off communication from family and friends. After the first 10 days, Brandon would call us about once a week. We longed for his calls and to hear his voice. We longed to hear that he was getting better. We wanted an end to this hell we were all trapped in. Family and friends prayed for Brandon and sent him notes almost daily. I remember him saying how much he appreciated everyone's encouragement, but to please stop sending the notes. His roommates were starting to build resentment towards him. Some of them had not received a single note during their stay. Some people have no one fighting in their corner and are alone. I know that Brandon felt tremendous guilt that he had an army of people loving on him. He felt shame for his addiction.

Brandon came home from rehab different than when he left. He seemed clear minded. It's a beautiful memory of him being healthy. His smile was back! His eyes were simply beautiful. I remember all of us being so happy that he was home. He was so loved! Brandon shared stories of the friends he had made in Florida. He met guys who were raised on the street and were abused in ways that are unspeakable. He met guys who have never experienced being in a family of love with a dad, mom, or siblings. They seemed to not have a chance even from the beginning of their lives. Guys who never heard of Jesus. I had the pleasure of meeting some of his buddies at the local meetings. I cherish those memories because it was at those meetings my heart felt their pain, and their real life struggles. They needed each other, and they raised their hands to each other for help. My favorite part of the meetings were when they received 'chips of sobriety': newcomer, 30 days, 60 days, 1 year, 20 years. It was encouraging to see victory! We were cheering on team members in the game of life. They were supporting and encouraging each other through a common spirit. Sometimes no words were needed to understand their friendship and support. Sometimes a hug, a handshake, or a smile was enough. Together they seemed stronger. They shared in their defeats, too. If someone relapsed and was back in rehab or back on the streets using, they talked about that. I remember one day Brandon came home and shared that he had bumped into a close friend who had relapsed. He was discouraged and worried for him. Brandon said many times to us that there are two places that he would end up if he continued to use drugs – in prison or dead. That was his reality and as hard as it was, it was ours too. He had a lot to lose. I'm so proud of my son for fighting so hard.

Brandon fought dark thoughts in his mind. Many times he shared his feelings of shame and guilt. He fought lies in his head that told him that he wasn't good enough, that he was worthless, and that people were against him. Were his thoughts influenced by medicine he was taking or by Satan's whispers of lies and deception? Satan's plan is to prey on us when we are physically or spiritually weak.

I remember Brandon asking me why people were curious to know the details of 'what' a person is addicted to. He went on to question, 'Does the type of addictive substance really matter?' His conclusion was that people are just nosey and the details don't help them care any more or less. This leads me back to the sensitive question that I've been asked, "How did Brandon become addicted to heroin." At the end of the day does the how really matter? There are so many paths that lead to addiction. Curiosity should not be the end of discussion. But I do know, addiction affects every race, religion, and status quo. It does not discriminate, and it is an ugly evil that comes to destroy lives.

How have we arrived at the place where we are losing thousands upon thousands every year to addiction? How do we help the addict? How do we help the loved ones of the addict? My answer is on our knees humbly asking our Lord for His wisdom and healing touch. We need Him.

So how did Brandon get through his years of struggles, testing, and temptations? He leaned a lot on friends, in both good and bad ways. He followed what the world offered him at times. He loved his wife and child. And he loved his family. We hold precious memories of my husband talking with Brandon on the drive home from AA meetings, pleading with Brandon to lean on Jesus for His strength, and Brandon looking at him with tears in his eyes saying, 'Dad, if you only knew how much I do.' Or my husband catching him in the kitchen with ear buds in his ears, back turned away from him with arms raised high to the heavens singing 'Chain Breaker'. Memories of us sitting in meetings with him talking about the never-ending love of God are where we know his real strength came from! We had many conversations with him about God. My son was close to the Lord. He understood God's love. He understood his struggles in the flesh, and that God didn't push him away. He knew he needed God. And he walked closely with Him. His first tattoos when he turned 16 read 'FEAR GOD'. These tattoos were huge letterings. FEAR on one forearm and GOD on the other forearm. It was bold! He took some backlashing from those tattoos. Some coaches and teachers questioned why he would fear God, and why he didn't tattoo 'Love God.' I think Brandon had a sense of GOD being GOD, one to be feared and one who is love.

Lost

On one side of the world, you have a young man battling addiction, and on the other side you have his family and friends hurting from watching him struggle and not being able to save him. I say 'world' because that's how it felt at times. Brandon was on one side of the world and we were on the other. He had his 'life' to work out and live out, and it was distant from us in many ways. He didn't let us in on the 'addiction' struggles. He actually pushed us away when he was actively using. We could talk about God, his child, his every day 'stuff', but he didn't trust us enough to talk about his personal addiction. Maybe that was because he knew we didn't fully understand. We tried to understand. I know he felt judged. Believe me, we wanted to help him, but we just didn't know how.

My husband recalls the time he called Brandon's family doctor to let him know that Brandon was abusing his pain medications. Doran felt tremendous guilt when he learned that the doctor refused to see Brandon after he had made that phone call. How can you refuse to see a patient that you know is struggling with an addiction? This particular doctor told Brandon that he had canceled too many appointments and therefore was no longer a patient. Brandon didn't know that we called his doctor. So did our intervening cause a complete shut off from his doctor? There were many days that we just didn't know what to do. Our countenance became weary. I became unraveled.

My family is my heart. My husband, daughter and son own a lot of it. I can't possibly describe why I am so crazy about them. There's just too much to say, and I'd need to write another book! I am sure most mothers are wildly crazy about their children. But one of the hardest things I have ever experienced in my life was watching my son suffer, and not being able to do anything about it.

I tried various ways to cope with my pain. I went to meetings with other mothers who had children fighting addiction, but after each meeting I felt worse. Someone always had a situation more desperate than mine. Always! And what I found as we went around the room sharing our child's struggles, was that no one could breathe life into my soul. No one had answers to help Brandon or to help me. I became accustomed to words like, 'be tougher on him', 'you're enabling him', 'he has to want it not you', or the worse one for me was 'he has to hit rock bottom'. I left many meetings feeling like I picked up more burdens from others than releasing my own. I know that sounds selfish, but I was trying to keep my head above water and move forward each day. People's advice sometimes caused pain because we were exhausting Plan A, Plan B, and all the way to Plan Z. It's fair to say that what works for one, doesn't work for all. We tried hard. I had zero control over Brandon's addiction, and I was desperate to save him. My heart was broken in a million pieces.

Nighttime was the hardest. The chances of him doing harm to himself seemed greater at night, and I wrestled with my thoughts. I remember several nights after he was asleep, going to his room and kneeling at his bed to pray over him. I would pray for his healing as I watched his chest rise and fall as he slept. I was so full of worry and fear. I knew he was so sick. This is when the habit of a strong glass of vodka and cranberry juice became my remedy to fall asleep. I just wanted to rest and not think. I did this for a few years and sometimes added a glass or two of wine. It worked for a while, but every morning, I had to deal with my feelings. I was losing my son right in front of me, and I couldn't stop it. Isn't it ironic that I turned to substance for relief as I watched my son battle substance abuse? I asked myself why 'he' turned to a substance? What was he needing relief from?

I turned to my family for support, but they were just as torn and broken as me. We couldn't really help each other through the pain. We all had our own ideas of what would turn Brandon around, and we seemed to frustrate each other at times for not 'doing things' the way the other thought it should be done. Many times division set in. I turned to my friends who always had time to listen and pray. They were praying for us all. I am so thankful for them, but I still felt like no one really truly understood. How could they? This was my son. *No one had the power to change my situation.* I was deeply tormented with fear.

My walk with Jesus was mainly prayers crying out to save my son. I wasn't reading the Bible much, and I went to church to worship at times that were convenient for me. You know, slipping into church service to worship, hearing encouraging words, and applying what I heard to my life for a day or so. I may have looked like a Christian, but I wasn't walking close to Jesus in my heart. I was walking in fear, and Brandon's battle was taking me under. It's only in looking back that I realize I was fighting with human solutions, human remedies, and human logic, not by the divine revelations and power that can only come from God.

Rescued

It was early one morning, the summer before Brandon passed that my life changed. I remember hearing my husband in the shower as I laid in bed crying out to the Lord to heal Brandon. I was literally crying The Lord's Prayer over and over and over again. I didn't know what else to pray. Every time I came to the passage, 'thy will be done, on earth as it is in heaven' I broke down in immense tears and sorrow. I know I prayed it 4 or 5 times that morning. It was a prayer that was breaking down 'my will' and submitting it to the Lord's. For the first time, I began praying in a way that I was giving my son to Jesus. I surrendered and I began to trust him with Brandon. I alone had no power. I had no answers. I knew that the Lord did! This wasn't the first time I had given Brandon over to the Lord in my heart. When he was 10 years old he was on life support at Hershey Medical fighting meningitis. That night we were told that Brandon may not make it through the night and if he did, he may lose some of his extremities. Doctors just didn't know the outcome. I remember bowing my head, laying my hands on his little body and saying 'Lord, I trust you and he belongs to you.' My walk with the Lord was closer when this illness happened, and I remember the Lord bringing those memories of Brandon in Hershey back to me 10 years later. I was fighting for his life again. And the peace that He gave me when Brandon was in Hershey Medical is the same peace that overcame me that morning. It's indescribable.

It was when I cried out to God in desperate helplessness that I developed a closeness to God that I have never had before. God literally came down and met me in my despair. He put his arms around me and gave me comfort. He met me in my place of pain and in my place of weakness. I surrendered everything to Him and I finally felt peace. I know that I am only strong because of Him.

From that morning on, I stopped turning to God last and started turning to Him first. I surrendered all of me. I pray my heart out to God. I empty myself to Him. I share my deepest hurts, my disappointments, my longings, my hopes, my fears - all of it. I share my joys and victories! I share it all. I read His word every day, meditating on His promises, His love, His assurances that He is with me, carrying me throughout each day. He is carrying me. He is carrying my family. He is carrying Brandon. My home is filled with spiritual music. I seek Him. I had cried out to many people over the course of Brandon's battle, but it was only when I cried out to the Lord, that He could fill me up. He is the only one that fills me up with His love and His peace! He's the only one! I was so close to seeking outside counseling. Maybe it would have helped, but I am so thankful that the great physician, our Lord Jesus Christ is my best friend. He knows everything about me and still loves me. He has never ever left my side. I don't even need to use words to explain myself to Him. He already knows, and He saved my life. I am so thankful! I need God. I am dependent on Him.

In the late summer, my family started attending a weekly prayer meeting with folks from Africa. We are so thankful for their love and friendship. They took us under their wings and taught us how to walk closely with Jesus. They stopped by our house to pray, they read scriptures on the phone, and they loved us like family. We fasted, broke bread together, and began to heal spiritually. We were hurting on the inside and only the Lord can heal us on the inside. My faith in Jesus increased as they walked the hard journey with me. My family grew stronger through their encouragement in God's word, not from their own personal opinions. This was the first time I understood the importance of feeding my spirit through the Bible. This was the first time I understood feeding my spirit through prayer and fasting. When fear starts to rear its ugly head in my life, I have learned to lean into Jesus. Their friendship encouraged my faith. I repeatedly needed to give my son over to God, to submit myself to His will and not mine. To this day, I continue to ask the Lord to remove my fears and replace it with His trust. It isn't always easy, but God's love for me is great! I intentionally set my mind on Jesus. It is where I find my peace. I know how He rescued me, and I know He will rescue you.

I remember thinking a lot about Jesus's mother, Mary. A mother watching her son suffer. Her son was perfect and loving, and yet hated by men. She watched him beaten and hung on a cross to save the world. I can't imagine her pain, but I know that she understands mine. And as I was relating to Mary's love, I found myself looking at Jesus as a mother looking at her broken son. The more I thought about Mary, the more I was drawn to her son, Jesus. I was drawn to Him as a child, a man, a person, but also as a son of God our LORD. A son so very loved by our Lord, who understands my pain.

One morning as I was praying, the Holy Spirit gave me these words. He knows everything that I have gone through and everything I am feeling. May these words bless you:

Where is my mind
50 Percent of the time?
Jesus I've lost my mind-
Jesus can you help me find it?

It's not in my cell phone, it's not on TV, it's not on the computer and yet it's all I see!

It's not with my best friend or my partner in crime. It's not with my lovely daughter who I am with a lot of times.
It's not with my broken son though I carry his weight around.
And it's not at the movies, the concerts or videos on TV.
It's not at my beach vacation, the getaway at the cabin or even the beautiful sea.
But where God oh where God can my mind be? Please help me find it, I just need to see.

It's not in my stylish shoes and latest fashion that I'm wearin'.
It's not in the bottle of wine although it helps me stop carin'.
And it's not in the Advil PM, Tylenol AM and it's not on the street!
Oh Lord I've looked, and I've searched in high and low places, to things and to people, to stars to the moon
but Lord it's not filling me up.
I just don't know what to do!
Please Lord help me find my peace, my rest, my tranquility.
I need you dear Lord oh please deliver me!
POWER IS OFF

AND then I pray.

AND then I open your word!

AND oh praises and Hallelujah I have finally found my Soul!!!

OH but Lord I have found it! I found it in YOU! You have opened my eyes and made me anew!
Sweet prayers in the morning, your word at noon, and talking to you Lord all day long it's what carries me through!
I'm focusing on the ONE and ONLY and most powerful YOU!
For you are the creator the mastermind of it all! You are the one true God, my miracle working King!
You created me and formed me and said you are pleased!
You've delivered me from this world and from my crazy mixed up head!
Abba Abba Abba - you are my dad!

You are my peace maker for that I am so grateful.
I will come to you praising only you and thanking only you --for our closeness that we have.

YOU fill my mind with your spirit and with your love. Yes it's so true!
You fill me up and only you give me perfect joy and peace beyond compare.
I walk in faith and not in fear - thank you thank you Jesus, thank you Jesus and Amen!

Jesus I am free! I am not crazy! I have not lost my mind!
For your blood paid the price and victory is MINE.
POWER IS ON!

One week later – I said my final goodbye to my son.

My world changed.

Although I always feared the possibility of overdose, I truly didn't believe it would happen to Brandon. For you see, I know my God who makes men out of dust. I know my God who can feed 5000 people with 5 loaves & 2 fish. I know my God who causes the blind to see. I know my God who walks on water. I know my God who raised Lazarus from the dead. And I know my God who gave His ONLY son Jesus to SAVE a sinful world so that we could be with Him forever. And I know that same miracle, all powerful, loving God could have physically healed Brandon if He willed it to be. And every day for the last 8 years, I was waiting on that miracle in Brandon's life. I was hoping and praying that addiction would no longer hold its devastating power over my son. So many were praying for Brandon, and we all had faith that the Lord was going to heal him. I remember being at a prayer meeting once, not even thinking about Brandon and saying the powerful name of Jesus over and over. I heard an audible voice in my head say, 'I will heal your son'. So I was waiting for the day when the Lord was going to put His hand on Brandon to physically heal him. Brandon did get his perfect healing from God! It just wasn't the physical touch here on earth that I had expected. He's in heaven with Jesus, where he is perfect.

The Lord does not leave me alone in my pain. He does not let me stay in my brokenness of heart. He continues to bring His gentle comfort and powerful healing to me. I need Him. I will always need Him. And I find peace knowing He holds my son until that wonderful day that I can hold him myself. The healing for my family and friends continues to seem supernatural at times. My faith is strong because I trust Jesus. He has delivered me from fear. He holds me and I trust Him.

Although Brandon lost his physical battle, he holds salvation (eternal life) because he asked Jesus to forgive him of his sins and to be Lord of his life. He was baptized when he was 17 years old. What a beautiful memory I will hold forever! Brandon knew that He needed Jesus, and he did not fight his battles alone. A few days after he passed, my husband found his Bible. Brandon had highlighted scriptures that were encouraging him. He was walking closer to the Lord than we realized. I am so thankful!

"Come to me, all you who are weary and burdened, and I will give you rest. Take my yoke upon you and learn from me, for I am gentle and humble in heart, and you will find rest for your souls. For my yoke is easy and my burden is light." (Matthew 11:28-30)

The Lord loves me through memories. The last time I saw Brandon was on a Wednesday afternoon, the week before he passed. I prayed with him, asking the Lord for help. We said "I love you", and hugged. It was one of his very warm hugs. His hugs were the best. Memories of my son come at random times making it hard to always hide my emotions, but I love my memories. I think God gives us memories to remind us of what we have to look forward to again someday. I am thankful for all of them, even the bad ones. I don't dwell on the bad ones though because I protect my spirit. I was able to watch Brandon as a husband, a father, a brother, an uncle, and my son. Uncle B was always making a big deal about his nephew, Cash. He was crazy about him. My son is in so many of my memories. He is my son whom I cherish. From my womb to my heart, he will always be a part of me. I miss him very much.

Brandon's son Jace will always remind me of my son. He carries his blue eyes, long eye lashes and charismatic personality. Jace was almost 3 years old when his daddy passed, but he has memories that amaze us all. Recently we took Jace to the doctor, and Jace was asked if he had any brothers or sisters at home because he could be contagious. Jace, not answering the question, very matter of fact stated, 'My daddy is in heaven with Jesus". The doctor stopped in his tracks and didn't know what to say. Jace rambled off something like "Yeah and I'm going to see him again someday." Who knows what seeds Jace is planting for Jesus! He is shining for his daddy and for Jesus! The blessings just keep flowing from that child!

It is very painful knowing that my husband, Doran, hurts so deeply over the loss of our son. Doran is an amazing husband and father! I want Brandon to be here with his dad; fishing, playing pool, or just hanging out as buds. Doran and Brandon had something very special, and I know that he misses him every single day. There's just something very deeply sad for me knowing that Brandon is not here with his dad. Doran remembers surrendering to the idea that there's nothing left for him to do for Brandon. He hangs on to the words of David in 2 Samuel who after losing his son said, "I will go to him, but he will not return to me." (2 Samuel 12:23)

We will go to Brandon one day for eternity in heaven. We will go to him. For now, Doran is my rock. I don't think I could love him any more than I do right now. I love him so much.

It is very hard watching my daughter, Danielle, hurt so deeply. She lost her only brother, her only sibling. She lost her close friend who shares her childhood memories. She loves him as only an older sister can – one that always looked out for him since the day he was born. She spoiled him rotten! She was 7 months pregnant when Brandon passed. On Christmas Eve, December 24, 2017 Danielle gave birth to Kai (Bear). He was an 8 pound, beautiful baby boy! Kai's arrival brought 'life' and healing to our family. We all believe that Kai has a little piece of his Uncle B in him. His precious life brought joy. At 6 months of age, Kai was diagnosed with Ocular Motor Apraxia. It's a condition that doctors know very little about. It is extremely rare. We were told that Kai would most likely need a wheel chair or cane to walk. Well, can I brag about the Lord's hand on this child, and say that Kai Bear is not only walking (without assistance) but is on his way to running to catch up with his older brother, Cash! We keep our hands raised in praise to our Lord for His healing touch, and we stay on our knees in prayer asking for His continual protection.

It's hard knowing that my grandson, Jace will grow up without the presence of his daddy. Brandon was so proud of his son, and I know at times fought harder because of him. I hold beautiful memories of him playing Legos on his bed, swimming in our pool laughing, and sitting in our kitchen dunking Oreo cookies in milk. We will continue to talk about his daddy, and his daddy's love for him. Jace will have to wait to see his daddy again, but we will all make sure that he understands how much his daddy loves him.

My daughter in law, Erika was the first person called to the scene when Brandon's body was found in his car. Brandon was the love of her life at an early age. My heart aches that she saw him. She stood by him through a lot, and I am thankful that she walks closely with the Lord. Her faith is strong, and she walks as a woman that knows she will see her husband again someday!

Watching my loved ones hurt is not easy, but I have learned to take my hurts to my Father. I raise them up to Him in my prayers knowing and trusting that He is more than enough to touch them, to heal them in ways that only He can. My calling is to love on them in ways that He leads me. I continually ask Him for wisdom and to truly understand what "His will on earth" means in my life. I approach Him with confidence because He has never let me down, ever! I trust Him with those I love. I trust Him with everything!

My family walks closer with Jesus since Brandon has passed. My husband, my daughter, my son in law, Brandon's wife and son, grandparents, cousins, nieces, nephews, uncles, aunts, close friends, and even acquaintances have grown closer to Jesus. Only a God of love could heal hearts through loss and suffering in ways that He has done for us. We praise our Lord, and we all can't wait to see Brandon again! We all seem to be slowly 'moving forward' not leaving Brandon behind, but taking him with us every day in a secret place tucked deep down in our hearts.

And we just can't look at people the same.
They are more precious.
We can't look at the beauty of the world the same.
The sky holds more gemstones.
The ocean is more majestic.
The sunrise is more brilliant.
The sunsets are more magnificent.
And the moon, well the moon is breathtaking!
My family watches the moon every day.
Brandon loved the moon!
I love it that The Holy Spirit brings my family together through the moon.
That's what He does – He brings us together!
We stand in awe of our Lord's love!

Life is more precious, and we have peace that only comes from Jesus!

My grandson, Jace, and I recently had a conversation about God being our heavily Father. He is Jace's Father and mine, too. Jace thought this was interesting. After Jace thought for a couple of seconds, he quietly stated, "GG, my daddy died". I nodded fighting back tears, as he added, "He was sick." Then he asked the question I wasn't quite ready for him to ask me. He said, "Why did he get sick GG?" Oh the many questions of 'why'? I could have explained that he was prescribed addictive medicine that changed his brain and his thinking. I could have somehow explained to him that substances (such as alcohol, drugs, medication) can be tools for Satan to use to attack our mind. How would I have explained all of the possible reasons anyone becomes addicted to anything such as drugs, alcohol, food, sex, pornography, work, gambling and a mile long list of other harmful addictions or strongholds?

I sometimes feel that addiction is looked at as a 'choice' that is driven from a selfish act of rebellion which would indicate the person is to blame for their addiction. Addiction is said to be linked to hereditary genes. In both explanations, the person suffering from addiction seems to be the source of the disease. I would argue that Satan's battle ground is in our minds, and his attacks start there as well. The substances we take that affect our minds can have deep consequences. Satan has been whispering lies since the beginning of mankind. He whispers lies of deception reminding us of our discomfort, of our unhappiness, of our broken heartedness, of our misery, and he will tempt us to turn to the world for relief. We don't 'naturally' turn to our Lord for help. Jace is only five years old, so he's not ready for this heart to heart with me, but he will continue to hear that his bloodline comes from Jesus Christ. He is a child of the living God who holds power and victory over ALL! Battles are coming, they are inevitable. But Jesus has never lost a battle. Not one!

"You, children, are from God and have overcome the false prophets, because He who is in you is greater than he who is in the world."
1 John 4:4

We live in a crazy world and in crazy times. There are so many ideas about God, and the Lord isn't always talked about or even presented as truth. In some of Brandon's rehabilitation centers, they talked of a 'higher being', but never a firm truth of our Lord and Savior. Our world sells that 'The Lord' is a theory or that we hold the power of supremacy of a god in ourselves alone. Well, I have a burning passion to share about the Truth found in the Living Word of God. He is not a theory. He is very much alive, and He wants to be Lord of your life! I want to share the reality of God's love for you. And the reality of the Father, the Son, and the Holy Spirit as ONE!

'Love More' is my attempt to share what I have found to be true about my Lord and God. I'm the first to admit that I don't have all of the answers, but that's where my faith kicks in to trust God. He has laid on my heart some of the basic foundations of who He is and who He wants to be to you.

There are parts of my book that I've included for specific reasons. One is the story of Mary, Martha, and Lazarus. It's a time where Jesus felt the pain of His friends after their brother died. I know that He really knew how we felt when Brandon passed, and He still comforts us with His understanding. I remember thinking about that during some of my really hard days. I included the story about Judas in hopes of bringing an awareness of how we allow Satan to have a foothold on us when we act out on our sin. Judas loved money and was a thief. His sin opened a hole or a way for Satan to enter him. Towards the end of my book, I write about God's tremendous love for you as your personal creator. My heart was heavy when I wrote this section. A young teenage girl in a nearby town had taken her own life. I hurt for our young ones who live in a world where comparison is magnified through social media, and their self-worth is defined by others.

You are not made to be me, and I am not made to be you. We are all made in the image of God, and His creation is so unique in each one of us. You don't need to prove to anybody that you are somebody! I pray my book touches hearts to know the love that God has for every single one of His creations. We are spiritual creatures desiring to be filled with a spirit of love and acceptance. Our need to be at peace and to feel loved, can only come from the Lord's Spirit. It can never be filled by the world. You are a child of The King!

Our Lord God is supernatural with divine powers. The Lord is not human. He is a personal God who lives inside of us, and I feel we have minimized His power in our lives. Somehow, we have made Him common as if He is on our level. I continually ask the Holy Spirit to help me to be sensitive to His direction, and to His supernatural divine power on my life. Here are a few of my own personal experiences with God and His supernatural touch:

The morning of Sunday, October 29, 2017 I went to church with my daughter and son in law. Brandon had been missing since the previous Friday evening and fear started to set in as I worshiped. Brandon had run off before, but never 3 days with no contact to anyone. He had turned his phone off, and we couldn't get in touch with him. He intentionally didn't want us to find him. At the end of church during worship, we were singing 'Death was arrested'. It's a victorious song of how our Savior paid the price over death, and we claim that same victory as ours. I had my hands raised in the air praising the Lord and singing when I heard a very evil laugh followed by rattling of chains and a door slamming. I looked at my son in law who was sitting beside me and asked if he heard the laugh. He had no idea what I was talking about. I heard the evil laugh again. I then asked my daughter, and she didn't hear anything either. I knew then that something was wrong. I had bowed my head and closed my eyes and had a vision of Brandon being chained up and taken away. I was afraid for him. I went home, put my grandson down for a nap, and received the call from my daughter in law. Brandon was found in a car less than a mile from her apartment. He had died of a heroin overdose earlier that morning.

Again, I feel like I don't have the words to explain my heart. I was broken. But at the same time my heart was broken, there was a fire that spread inside of me that went from my head down to my feet. I have never felt so much anger in my entire life! I went outside of my house to scream and cry. I remember picking up a rock and hesitating. It took every bit of self-control not to break every window in my house. If my grandson wasn't napping, I'm sure I would have smashed the glass in my family room. Brandon's earthly battle was over. And we lost. My anger was towards Satan. My rage was at his pathetic nature of harming, destroying, and killing others. I hate him. I know people aren't comfortable talking about him because he holds power, but he is no match for our Lord and Savior! Jesus has already won the victory over death and sin! His death and resurrection allows His Holy Spirit to live in me.

The first person I called was my husband. He was at work. He frantically left and headed straight to Brandon in total panic and fear. Doran remembers scrambling to get to the parking lot and seeing Brandon's car. A police officer was standing beside his car with the driver's door hanging open. Doran approached the officer and remembers saying, 'I'm his father. Is he gone?' The officer nodded 'yes'. Doran sat back down in his truck to try to gain strength and composure. He felt a deep remorse that somehow he had failed his son. Doran said that Brandon looked peaceful, like he had fallen asleep. This time there was no waking him. Doran hugged him. A billion tears. My daughter was the next call. SO much agony. So much pain.

So what does the evil one try to whisper in my ear today? How does he try to make me doubt and hold fear? How does he try and steal my joy? He has whispered lies that my son is in hell. He has whispered lies that Brandon is not a child of God. He has whispered lies of doubt of how could Brandon be in heaven if he was sinning. Fear has gripped me for most of my life. My mom passed when I was 8 years old from an illness, and I lived in fear when raising my children that something would happen to me or to them. I held fear of death, of being separated from those that I love. Fear is a liar, and it's a spirit that comes from Satan. The evil one whispers all lies and deception! And I fight those lies with the Word of God. I hold these truths for myself and I hold them for my son! Those chains that I heard rattling the Sunday when he passed weren't from Brandon being chained up, they were from his chains falling off!

Romans 3:23 *"For ALL have sinned and come short of the glory of God."* (I sin. Brandon sinned. We ALL sin.)

John 3:16, 17 *"For God so loved the world that He gave His one and only son. **That whosoever believeth in Him shall not perish, but have everlasting life.** For God sent not His son into the world to condemn the world, but that the world through Him would be saved."*
(Brandon believed in Jesus. They were friends.)

Ephesians 2:8 *"For it is by grace that you are saved, through faith – and this is not from yourselves, it is a gift from God."*
(We can't earn our salvation. No one can be good enough to enter heaven. It's a free gift to receive, and my son received that gift!)

The days after Brandon passed are fuzzy. Time was heavy and slow. I remember a lot of beautiful family and friends gathering around to hold us.

We had a small viewing for family and close friends the day before Brandon's celebration of life ceremony. Danielle and

I chose not to go. A handful of close friends wanted to see Brandon for closure. All of my memories of my son are of him alive. I know that he's not on earth, and yet I have a deep peace knowing that he's very much alive with my Lord. Jesus was able to give Brandon everything I could not. He's no longer in pain. He no longer is suffering. Jesus never left His side. That's what Jesus always does. He steps in and rescues. Love wraps us tight.

I hope to never forget the supernatural touch from the Holy Spirit. My family gathered at our house to plan Brandon's celebration of life ceremony with our pastor. We had reluctantly agreed to each speak at his ceremony, and I really did not want to speak. It was hard enough to carry a one on one conversation with someone. I couldn't imagine speaking in front of a large group of people. I remember praying to God, and telling Him that if He wanted me to do this, He would have to give me the words and the strength. The day before his service, the Lord gave me words to speak, but he also gave me a special gift.

When I woke up the day before Brandon's service, God had given me lion eyes. I'm not talking metaphorically. I mean He literally gave me lion eyes. When I blinked my eyes, I had the awareness of my eyes being as a lion. When I looked in the mirror, I looked normal, but when I blinked my eyes I could see lion's eye lashes and a lion's mane – I had lion eyes! The Lord spoke to my heart. He was going to be my strength at Brandon's celebration of life ceremony. When I was being overtaken with emotions, I would simply need to blink my eyes and breathe His breath. And true to His word, His breath filled me. I knew that His strength was inside of me, carrying me, speaking. I know it sounds crazy and I've only shared this with a few people, but the Lord gave me lion eyes. In a way, having lion eyes has helped me understand the concept of the Trinity. When I had the lion eyes, I wasn't a lion. I was very much a human with lion's eyes. The manifestation of His eyes strengthened my faith to understand His dimensional powers. I can't scientifically explain

His supernatural touches in my life, but I know it was very real. I am thankful for His hand on my life. He was my strength then, and He is my strength now.

On November 2, 2017 we gathered for Brandon's celebration of life service at a local church. Close to 600 people came out to love on us. We are blessed to live in a small town with people who love generously. We spoke about the love for my son, but the main focus of the evening was on the love of our Lord Jesus Christ and each other. The Lord totally orchestrated his service. We felt His presence. I only had the lion eyes for a few days, but they changed my life. I know that lion still lives in me, and when I become fearful or feel alone, I rely on Him. I believe in the supernatural God who loves me and who loves you. He will show you His love and His power, you just have to seek Him first before anything or anyone else. You just have to want Him.

Our family and a few friends gathered at our house after Brandon's service. I had received several text messages from friends that night who were at the service, remarking how they 'felt' the Holy Spirit during his service. So many were commenting about the sky, and that the moon had a radiance that had touched them. It was around 11pm when family, friends, and I decided to go outside to check out the moon. A beautiful sight was waiting for us all. The moon had shades of blue, orange, yellow, and red clouds twirling around it in a circular motion. Clouds of color! We watched in awe. We cried, we laughed, and we raised our hands to God. It was almost as if the beauty of the moon was just for us! It was a sign to us that Our Almighty Lord has all of us in His loving hands. The next day our neighbors shared that they heard us laughing. He was questioning his wife as to what could be going on. His wife thought we were experiencing laughter as a grief mechanism and a way to cope with our loss. I explained to him that our joy and laughter came directly from the Lord's hand. He was loving on us through His creation. We worship God, not the stars and moon, but His beautiful moon was testifying to us that night. He is so amazing and powerful! And the moon.....well, it will always be my favorite piece of art created by our Lord God. I hope to never underestimate the power of God's love manifested in people and in His creation.

The Lord has laid visions on my heart and in my mind. One vision is that He has given me gentle reminders as I'm talking with people of how we all are created by Him. When I look at people, He would remind me to look at the skeletal structure in their face. In other words, I had a sense of them without skin. It's not scary, it's a reminder that someday the flesh will be gone. Underneath our skin, we are all so very similar with bones and spirit. And as I reflect on the passing of the flesh, I look at each person having a soul. I think it's best to describe my vision as the Lord laying on my heart that what is on the outside of a person will pass quickly and is not the importance of the person. The real focus needs to be on who the persons Lord is on the inside. That is supernatural to me.

For years now, almost daily I see hawks. We live in an area with a lot of hawks. The hawk is a creature of prey. All day long, every day his sole purpose is to hunt down other animals to eat. The Lord laid on my heart the similarities of Satan. All day long, all night long his sole purpose is to kill, steal, and destroy. He studies our weaknesses, he studies our children, he is always looking to tempt us in order to lead us down the wrong path, and he whispers lies. His goal is to distance us from God. This awareness is not to instill fear in me, but to keep my heart open to the hurting, to us being under attack, and to those being deceived by lies spoken in their minds. That is supernatural to me.

Many times as I'm praying I have visions of our Lord seated on His throne and His son Jesus sitting beside Him. They are both in white and although I can't see their faces, they are sitting on a throne unified as one King! To me that is supernatural. I have visions or an awareness of angels descending in my house. I feel their presence when I'm praying or reading the word of God out loud. To me that is supernatural.

As I was writing this book, I had a continual vision of our Lord God moving through the clouds. He is always in motion moving gracefully. Every day I gain a clearer understanding of how much He loves you and me. I know that I'm only experiencing a tiny fraction of what His love really is for us! To me that's supernatural.

The title, 'Love More' comes from a conversation that Brandon and I had one evening when he was struggling. It was late at night and as we sat in my car, he was sharing some of his struggles. I prayed with him and remember encouraging him to look at himself instead of how other people are the cause for his conflicts. I asked him what would happen if he chose to look at himself and simply, 'Love More'. I remember asking him to love ridiculously, over the top, just a little bit more at times when he wanted to throw in the towel. That conversation ended with a beautiful smile and "Thanks Mom." The next morning he showed me the picture that he had painted of 'Love More' (cover of this book). It will always be a reminder for me to reach beyond the love I think I'm capable of giving, and to simply love more even if it's just a little bit more.

We all will take our final breath someday, but where your spirit goes after your physical death is a choice that I pray you understand. Death is serious. I ask the Lord to give you an open mindset to allow the gentle Holy Spirit to touch your heart, open your eyes to see the gift of life that He offers to give you, and that all veils be lifted for clearer understanding. I am purposing myself to pray for each person that reads this book. May you intentionally pursue Jesus to know Him as your close, personal Messiah. May His spirit draw you near to Him.

Before you read, will you say a simple prayer and ask God to reveal His truth to your heart?

Shalom (Peace)
Amy

Isaiah 55:6-12
"Seek the Lord while he may be found;
    call on him while he is near.
Let the wicked forsake their ways
    and the unrighteous their thoughts.
Let them turn to the Lord, and he will have mercy on them,
    and to our God, for he will freely pardon.
"For my thoughts are not your thoughts,
    neither are your ways my ways,"
declares the Lord.
"As the heavens are higher than the earth,
    so are my ways higher than your ways
    and my thoughts than your thoughts.
As the rain and the snow
    come down from heaven,
and do not return to it
    without watering the earth
and making it bud and flourish,
    so that it yields seed for the sower and bread for the eater,
so is my word that goes out from my mouth:
    It will not return to me empty,
but will accomplish what I desire
    and achieve the purpose for which I sent it.
You will go out in joy
    and be led forth in peace;
the mountains and hills
    will burst into song before you,
and all the trees of the field
will clap their hands."

LOVE
MORE

Life is fast and seems to change almost daily.
Nothing seems certain.
Nothing seems concrete.
There seems to be no absolutes.
Your neighbors have opinions.
Your friends have opinions.
And you have your own personal opinions as to what is truth.
Who is right and who is wrong?
The world encourages you to base opinions as your personal foundation of truth.
Yet this so-called truth has created a world of uncertainties, of doubts, of fears, and of anxieties.
It's a foundation that shifts and changes, leaving us on uncertain ground.
A foundation that can lead to total destruction in your life.
This changing world can be a scary place for people who trust only in things, other people, or themselves.
What is Truth?

How did the world begin? Who created you? Why are there good and evil? Why are you here?
What is your purpose? Is there a God? Where is He? Who is He? Does God love me?
Why is there so much brokenness? Is there life after death and does it really matter?

Who do I believe?

You deserve the truth!
The truth is much more than your feelings that change with
your circumstances.
The truth does not change from day to day.
The truth is found in the Word of God. It's a book about Adonai,
Yeshua, the Holy Spirit, and you!

Adonai, Yeshua, and the Holy Spirit are ONE GOD!
He is our TRUTH, our foundation, and He is revealed to us in the
living Word of God!
Those who trust in God will have hope and confidence.
He is the one true constant in our chaotic world.
His Word is always true. His power is absolute. And He always
keeps His promises!

ONE GOD –
THE GREAT I AM

The Great I AM, the One who created ALL of life itself, is
supernatural!
He is ADONAI! He is GOD!
Adonai (God), Yeshua (Jesus), and the Holy Spirit are manifested
in ONE Supreme Being.
I AM. ALMIGHTY God!

Before daylight and nighttime, there is Adonai.
Before the sun, stars, and moon, there is Adonai.
Before all animals and people, there is Adonai.
Before time begins, there is ONE GOD and He is ONE LORD
over all!
He has always existed and will always exist forever!
He is immortal. He is not human.
Adonai is supernatural and everything begins with Him!
I AM. The LORD of all the earth!

Adonai moves like the wind in constant motion and sails high
above the earth,
and yet He is as close to you as your breath.
He never sleeps and keeps a watchful eye on His children.
I AM. Lord God most high!

How does Adonai reveal himself to you, if you can't see Him
with your eyes?

He reveals Himself to you through His Spirit, His Word, and prayers.
He whispers softly to your heart when you are alone with Him.
Trust your eyes to see His touches of greatness.
Trust your eyes to see His touches of beauty in nature and this vast world that you live in!
Trust your heart when you hear His voice of love for you.
I AM. Mystery!

Adonai is Holy and Almighty!
He is perfect in ALL ways!
He is righteous and full of endless grace.
He is kind, empathetic, and understanding.
He is everything good, wonderful, and amazing!
He loves you so very much!
I AM. Holy!

Adonai has strong emotions and is so very personal.
Joy, happiness, anger, sadness all belong to our Lord.
He knows your pain and understands you.
He loves you so closely.
He wants the very best for you because He loves you like no person in the world can ever love you.
I AM. The Living God!

Adonai is LORD! He is Ruler over everything and holds the greatest power of all!
NO ONE can be compared to His greatness!
He is supernatural with divine powers.
I AM. Worthy!

Adonai is the wisest and can only act in perfect ways!
He knows everything and can do everything!
He answers to no one and is in full control of everything, everywhere!

The Lord Adonai knows everything about *you* and everything about the world that He created!
You can trust Him because He knows the past, present, and the future. He does not have any uncertainty about you or this world.
This brings peace and trust.
I AM. Knowledge and Truth!

Why Did Adonai Create MANKIND?

He took the dust from the earth into His hands and formed man.
He breathed on him and filled man with His breath.
Supernaturally!
Adonai is a God of relationships. He created you out of His love
for you.
He created you with a desire to have a close relationship with
Him.
Your creator is LIFE, and He is LOVE!
I AM. Father!

Adonai made man physical (hands, feet, and body) and spiritual
(spirit and soul).
You have a body, mind, and soul. Three parts and yet one.
Out of His love, you are given a choice of free will.
A free will to choose Him as the LORD of your life.
I AM. Creator!

The first man created was Adam, and the first woman was Eve.
They were His family.
Adonai came down from heaven and enjoyed a closeness with
His family here on earth.
It was a relationship with perfect love.
Adonai provided a home for his family with delicious food,
beautiful trees and flowers, and amazing animals.
It was perfect!
They were happy!
I AM. Provider!

Adam was given authority from Adonai to take care for His beautiful garden. Eve was his helper.

They lived together in peace and love. It was a joy for them to care for His garden of paradise.

The authority that Adonai gave Adam came with one exception. Adonai told them to eat and enjoy all of the fruits in the garden, except for the fruits from the Tree of the Knowledge of Good and Evil.

Adam and Eve had free will with a choice.

All authority under the Lord Adonai comes with the choice to obey Him.

If they ate from the tree, *they would die*.

(Gen. 2:17)

They would be separated from God if they disobeyed.

Death means separation. Separation of the soul from God.

I AM. The Authority!

Satan is an evil, fallen angel from heaven.

He is wicked and was thrown out of heaven for his rebellion against Adonai.

He wants to be as God. He hates God and is full of pride. His purpose is to kill, steal, and destroy everything and everyone.

The Bible refers to him as the evil one, the ruler of this world, the god of this age, and the prince of the power of the air.

He attacks Adonai's people.

He is a murderer from the beginning and a liar.

Adonai allows him to live on earth, and he lived in the garden with Adam and Eve.

He wanted to kill Adam and Eve. He wants to kill mankind.

He wanted them to disobey Adonai and to become separated from the Lord.

He came to kill and destroy their family.

In the garden, Satan spoke lies to Eve.

His lies tempted her to question Adonai.

He influenced her to eat from the tree and disobey Adonai.

Satan is a liar, and he whispers lies to you and me.

Our minds and thoughts are the battleground of his attacks.
I AM. The Lord, the King!

Adam and Eve had the perfect loving Father.
They enjoyed the physical presence of Adonai. They were His family.
They had everything perfect, and yet they chose to disobey Him.
Eve disobeyed Adonai and ate the fruit from the tree.
Adam disobeyed and ate it, too.
Adam and Eve's decision to disobey changed their relationship with God.
They were filled with feelings of shame. Guilt and shame come from sin.
They covered themselves and hid in the garden from Adonai.
I AM. The Lord, the Judge!

Their relationship with their Father, Adonai, became broken.
Adonai took animals, which He dearly loved, and sacrificed them.
He sacrificed His creation to clothe Adam and Eve. It was a type of blood sacrifice.
Adam and Eve were Adonai's family, but because they chose to disobey their Father, sin separated them from Him.
From that time and until now, all humans are born with the curse of sin.
We are born with a desire to be independent from Adonai.
Sin separates us from Him.
Adonai is a sovereign Lord, and sin cannot go unpunished.
He is the Holy Lord, one to honor and obey.
Adonai's love didn't change because of Adam and Eve's disobedience.
He is a relational Lord of love.
He loves His children!
He came down from heaven out of love, to save us from this curse of death and separation.
We were influenced by sin, we chose sin, and yet our Lord chose to save us.
I AM. Sovereign!

ONE GOD –
Yeshua – God Is Salvation

Yeshua (Jesus) is 100 percent God and 100 percent man.
Yeshua was conceived and born by his mother Mary and by the power of the Holy Spirit.
Yeshua was not conceived from a human father.
He is supernatural with Divine powers (super powers)!
The Lord Adonai sent Yeshua, His only Son, down from heaven as a baby to live with us on earth.
He sent Yeshua to break the curse of sin, the curse of death that separates us from Adonai.
Yeshua came to save us!
He came to teach us how to love Adonai and how to love others.
He shared many secrets about Adonai, angels, heaven, hell, and you!
I AM. Yeshua!

As a man, Yeshua experienced many of the same things that we do.
He had a family with a mother, father, sisters, and brothers.
He grew up in a Jewish community learning the ways of his culture.
He learned how to be a carpenter by trade.
Yeshua was here on earth as a man.
He knows exactly how it feels to be human.
I AM. Son of God and Man!

Yeshua told everyone that He is God! That He is the Messiah!

He did MANY amazing things to prove that He is God!
He walked on TOP of water. (He has Supernatural Powers!)
He fed 5,000 people with just 2 fish and 5 loaves of bread! (He has Supernatural Powers!)
And Yeshua was the most excellent doctor!
He healed the blind to see! (He has Divine Powers!)
He healed the lame to walk. (He has Divine Powers!)
He brought the dead back to life again! (He has Divine Powers!)
People were waiting for hundreds of years for Yeshua to come to earth.
Adonai promised to send Yeshua (Messiah), and He did!
He *proved* to mankind that He is God.
But the people still denied Him, and they didn't believe Him as the Son of Adonai.
He is Adonai's son! He is supernatural possessing Adonai's divine power!
I AM. The Lord Your Healer!

Yeshua had chosen twelve close friends.
They left their families, jobs, and possessions to serve others with Him. He loved them.
Just like your friends, they talked, laughed, cried, and were very close.
He taught them to heal others, forgive others, and most importantly, to love others through His name.
He sought after people who needed help and love.
He sought out the hurting and the broken hearted, and they sought Him.
All were blessed by His love and His powers.
I AM. Faithful Friend!

One of the greatest miracles Yeshua performed was bringing His close friend, Lazarus, back from the dead.
Yeshua was close friends to two sisters, Mary and Martha, and their brother Lazarus.
Yeshua loved their family.

Lazarus became very sick and died.

This was devastating to Mary and Martha.

Yeshua cried with them as they mourned for their brother. He loved his friends.

His divine power raised Lazarus from the dead (three days after he died).

He proved that He is the Son of Adonai.

I AM. Merciful!

Mary and Martha hosted a dinner to honor Yeshua for bringing their brother Lazarus back to life.

I can only imagine their hearts being so full of happiness and joy.

Martha served the meal while Mary took expensive perfumed oil and poured it on Yeshua's feet.

She spread the oil with her hair. Mary loved him so much.

Judas, one of Yeshua's twelve closest friends, was at the dinner.

He scolded her for using the expensive perfume.

Judas was interested in the oil for money.

He was in charge of the money box and had stolen from it.

He was a traitor and a thief.

Satan entered Judas, the one who ultimately betrayed Yeshua for, 30 coins.

I AM. Worthy!

Yeshua's popularity and following became very great after the miracle of Lazarus.

His enemies became desperate.

They didn't want people to follow Yeshua, the Son of God.

Yeshua spoke directly to the high priests, church leaders, and those who esteemed themselves to be higher than everyone else.

They loved the outward traditions of religion and not the inward change of the heart that comes from Yeshua.

Yeshua says in Matthew 5:17 *"Don't think that I have come to abolish the Torah [Old Testament] or the Prophets. I have come not to abolish but to complete."*

Yeshua knew that they desired favor from people instead of favor from God.

He knew their hearts were full of self-righteousness and pride.

They wanted Yeshua to be someone that could physically fight and defeat their enemies as a president or captain that goes to war.

They wanted the son of God to kill and destroy their personal enemies.

Some people hated Him for being our loving God.

Their hearts grew from a passion of hate to an obsession to kill.

I AM. The Lord Our Defense!

As the time was close for Yeshua to become our sacrifice, He spent time in prayer with His Father, Adonai.

He knew the punishment that was coming, and that it was going to involve great physical pain.

He knew that He was the only one who could break the curse of sin and death on mankind.

He knew He was the only one to give us life eternal with no separation from our Lord and our loved ones.

I AM. Sacred Sacrifice!

Luke 22:42-44 reads,
"Father, if you are willing,
take this cup away from me;
still, let not my will
but yours be done."
There appeared to him an angel from heaven giving him strength,
and in great anguish he prayed more intensely, so that his sweat
became like drops of blood falling to the ground."

Yeshua was killed by the men and women who hated Him.

He died a very painful death when they nailed Him on a cross.

"The governor's soldiers took Yeshua into the headquarters
building, and the whole battalion gathered around him.
They stripped off his clothes and put on him a scarlet robe,

wove thorn-branches into a crown and put it on his head,
and put a stick in his right hand.
Then they kneeled down in front of him and made fun of him:
'Hail to the King of the Jews!'
They spit on him
and used the stick to beat him about the head.
When they had finished ridiculing him,
they took off the robe, put his own clothes back on him
and led him away to be nailed to the execution stake.
As they were leaving, they met a man from Cyrene named Simon;
And they forced him to carry Yeshua's execution-stake.
When they arrived at a place called Golgotha (which means 'place
of the skull'),
they gave him wine mixed with bitter gall to drink;
but after tasting it, he would not drink it.
After they had nailed him to the stake,
they divided his clothes among them by throwing dice.
Then they sat down to keep watch over him there.
Above his head they placed the written notice stating the charge
against him,
THIS IS YESHUA
THE KING OF THE JEWS
Then two robbers were placed on execution-stakes with him, one
on the right and one on the left.
People passing by hurled insults at him, shaking their heads
and saying, "So you can destroy the Temple, you can, and rebuild
it in three days?
Save yourself, if you are the Son of God,
and come down from the stake!"
Likewise, the head priest jeered at him,
along with the Torah-teachers and elders,
"He saved others, but he can't save himself!"
"So he's King of Israel, is he?
Let him come down now from the stake! Then we'll believe him!"
"He trusted God?

So, let him rescue him if he wants him!
After all, he did say, 'I'm the Son of God'!"
Even the robbers nailed up with him insulted him in the same way.
From noon until three o'clock in the afternoon, all the Land was
covered with darkness.
At about three, Yeshua uttered a loud cry, 'My God! My God! Why
have you deserted me?'
On hearing this, some of the bystanders said, "He's calling for Elijah."
Immediately one of them ran and took a sponge, soaked it in
vinegar,
put it on a stick and gave it to him to drink.
The rest said, "Wait! Let's see if Elijah comes and rescues him."
But Yeshua, again crying out in a loud voice, yielded up his spirit."
Matthew 27: 27-50

Adonai could have stopped them. Yeshua could have stopped
them.
His love took all of our sins on Himself.
His love saves us from death and gives us freedom to live!
Yeshua chose to be our sacrifice and to die on the cross for our sins.
He loves you so much!
I AM. The Cure!

Yeshua overcame the sin that separates us from Adonai, and He
defeated the enemy who hates us.
Does this mean that you have to live a perfect, sinless life in
order to be Adonai's child?
No, you aren't perfect. No one is perfect accept Yeshua.
When you admit that you need to be saved because you can't
save yourself, He will save you.
When you admit that you have sinned, He will forgive you.
When you believe Yeshua is the son of Adonai, you will have
everlasting life.
You will never die.

You are free to live your life with Him.
You are free from any chains (sins) that hold you down.
Yeshua saves you from death – from being separated from God.
Yeshua saves you from hell!
I AM. Salvation!

HELL Is Real

Hell is a terrible, horrific, tortuous place for those who don't believe with faith that Yeshua is the son of God, and that He is the only way to break your curse of sin.
It is a lie that a loving God will not condemn those who do not accept His son Jesus as Lord.
God loves you so much that He made a way to escape hell. You have the choice to choose Yeshua as Lord.
It is a lie that there are many ways to heaven.
The Word is clear that there is only one way to heaven, and it is through Yeshua the Messiah.
It is a lie that you can go to heaven by being a good person.
We are righteous only through Yeshua.
Yeshua is the only way to eternal life.
Adonai is a just LORD, and He cannot forgive the choice of denying Yeshua, His son.
I AM. The Way, The Truth, and The Life.

Those who die without knowing Yeshua as their Savior and friend will go to hell with Satan and his demons.
They will be alive in darkness and in suffering.
They will live in torment with gnashing of teeth.
They will be separated forever from Adonai and their loved ones.

"And whosoever was not found written in the book of life was cast into the lake of fire."
Revelation 20:15

"And fear not them which kill the body, but are not able to kill the soul; but rather fear him which is able to destroy both soul and body in hell."
Matthew 10:28

When you believe that Yeshua is the son of God, and admit that you need Him to save you from your sins, He will forgive you and save you!
We ALL are born with the curse to sin as soon as we enter the world. It's part of being human.
Yeshua died to set you free of that curse!
I AM. Jehovah!

Death has no power over Yeshua!
Three days after He died, He came out of the grave very much alive!
Satan thought he had won the battle over death when Yeshua was killed on the cross, but our Lord defeated death!
Hallelujah and praises to our Lord, He is very much alive!
Yeshua is alive and He holds the *power over death*!
His resurrection proved that no physical death is final.
I AM. The Eternal, All-Sufficient God!

"As they were going, some of the guards went into the city and reported to the head priest everything that had happened. Then they met with the elders; and after discussing the matter, they gave the soldiers a sizeable sum of money and said to them, 'Tell people, "His disciples came during the night and stole his body while we were sleeping." If the governor hears of it, we will put things right with him and keep you from getting in trouble.' The soldiers took the money and did as they were told, and this story has been spread about by the Judeans till this very day."
Matthew 28:11-15

Lies were told to cover up Yeshua's resurrection, and they are still being told today.

There are so many deceptions and lies created by the enemy, lies to keep you from knowing the truth of Yeshua.

Yeshua's friends witnessed Yeshua alive!
They had watched Him with their own eyes die on the cross.
How could He be alive?
He is the Son of the Great I AM! He is the Son of Adonai!
They were filled with extreme joy at seeing Yeshua again, very much alive!
Their faith and trust in Him became stronger than ever before!
There was full belief from His friends that He is the Son of Adonai, the Messiah.
I AM. Victory!

"After his death he showed himself to them and gave many convincing proofs that he was alive. During a period of forty days they saw him, and he spoke with them about the Kingdom of God. At one of these gatherings, he instructed them not to leave Jerusalem but to wait for 'what the Father promised, which you heard about from me. For John used to immerse people in water, but in a few days, you will be immersed in the Holy Spirit.'"
Acts 1:3-5

Yeshua told His friends to be happy that He was going back to heaven, because He would send them a gift!
He would send the Holy Spirit of God down from heaven.
The Holy Spirit is God (His breath) living INSIDE each of us!
Yeshua needed to leave earth and go back home to heaven with His Father to prepare a place in heaven for you and me.
Yeshua supernaturally rose up through the clouds to join His Father, Adonai, in heaven.
His friends praised Adonai in the Temple courts!
I AM. The Deliverer!

ONE God –
The Holy Spirit – God's Breath
(Ruach HaKodesh)

Since the very beginning of time, Adonai the Father, Yeshua His Son, and the Holy Spirit are One.

The Holy Spirit was with God since the beginning: *"In the beginning God created the heavens and the earth. The earth was unformed and void, darkness was on the face of the deep, and the Spirit of God hovered over the surface of the water." Genesis 1:1, 2*

The Holy Spirit is God in the Torah (Old Testament) and the New Testament.

He was with King David – A shepherd boy who slayed giants and was a great powerful king. *"Don't thrust me away from your presence, don't take your Holy Spirit away from me." Psalm 51:11*

He was with Moses – A great leader needing wisdom for his people. *"I will come down and speak with you there, and I will take some of the Spirit which rests on you and put it on them. Then they will carry the burden of the people along with you, so that you won't carry it yourself." Numbers 11:17*

He was with Daniel – He was given wisdom and power to interpret dreams. *"I have heard of you, that the Spirit of God is in you, and that light and understanding and excellent wisdom are found in you." Daniel 5:14 NKJV*

He was with Elijah and Elisha – Elijah went up to heaven in a whirlwind. *"The Spirit of Elijah does rest on Elisha." 2 Kings 1:15*

He was with Micah – Micah defends the rights of the poor against the rich and powerful, while looking forward to a world at peace centered on Zion. *"On the other hand, I am full of power by the Spirit of Adonai, full of justice and full of might to declare Jacob his crime, to Israel his sin." Micah 3:8*

The Holy Spirit holds power by which God accomplishes His purpose.
<u>He is fully God.</u>

Yeshua spoke that the Holy Spirit would fill us and speak truth to our hearts.
"When the counselor comes, whom I will send you from the Father – the Spirit of Truth, who keeps going out from the Father – he will testify on my behalf." John 15:26

Adonai, Yeshua and the Holy Spirit work as one!
"And I will ask the Father, and He will give you another comforting Counselor like me, The Spirit of Truth, to be with you forever." John 14:16

"Suddenly there came a sound from the sky like the roar of a violent wind, and it filled the whole house where they were sitting. Then they saw what looked like tongues of fire, which separated and came to rest on each of them. They were all filled with the Holy Spirit (Ruach HaKodesh) and began to talk in different languages, as the Spirit enabled them to speak. Now there were staying in Jerusalem religious Jews from every nation under heaven. When they heard this sound, a crowd gathered; they were confused, because each one heard the believers speaking in his own language. Totally amazed, they asked, "How is this possible? Aren't all these people who are speaking from the Galil? How is it that we hear them speaking in our native languages? We are Parthians, Medes, Elamites; residents of Mesopotamia, Y'hudah, Cappadocia, Pontus, Asia, Phrygia, Pamphylia, Egypt, the parts of Libya near

Cyrene; visitors from Rome; Jews by birth and proselytes; Jews from Crete and from Arab…! How is it that we hear them speaking in our own languages about the great things God has done?" Amazed and confused, they all went on asking each other, "What can this mean?" But others made fun of them and said, "They've just had too much wine!" Then Kefa stood up with the Eleven and raised his voice to address them: "You Judeans, and all of you staying here in Yerushalayim! Let me tell you what this means! Listen carefully to me!

These people aren't drunk, as you suppose – it's only nine in the morning. No, this is what was spoken about through the prophet Yo'el:

Adonai says:
"In the Last Days,
I will pour out from my Spirit upon everyone.
Your sons and daughters will prophesy,
your young men will see visions,
your old men will dream dreams.
Even on my slaves, both men and women,
will I pour out from my Spirit in those days;
and they will prophesy.
I will perform miracles in the sky above
and signs on the earth below-
blood, fire, and thick smoke.
The sun will become dark
and the moon blood
before the great and fearful Day of Adonai comes.
And then, whoever calls on the name of Adonai will be saved."
Acts 2: 1-21

When you read the Holy Bible and pray, you will hear the Holy Spirit guiding you with His wisdom and Truth!
The Holy Spirit's power comes to you through the living word of Adonai, the Bible.
As you read the Word, you will sense His presence.

Talk to Adonai in prayer, and you will sense that He is listening and cares about you!
This awareness comes from the Holy Spirit.
Stay quiet and listen for Him, and you will sense how much He loves you and is with you!
Obey Him and you will receive His many blessings that He wants to give you!
His power carries the Truth from your head to His changes needed in your heart.
Reading His word and praying—this is how you develop a deep relationship with Adonai, Yeshua, and the Holy Spirit.
I AM. Love!

YOU are made to have a relationship with our Lord Yeshua, a relationship that is as close as the one Adam and Eve had with Adonai, a relationship to walk and talk every day of your life with Him!
When you confess that Yeshua is Lord, and ask Him for forgiveness of your sins,
the Holy Spirit lives INSIDE of you!
I AM. The Lord Your Helper!

The Holy Spirit fills you with His love.
He is gentle and kind.
He offers you comfort, peace, and joy.
Only the Spirit of God can do the will of God.
I AM. Gentle!

The Holy Spirit speaks Truth to your heart and leads you in ways that you are to go.
He is all-powerful and is everywhere present. You are never alone for He stays so close to you!
He is the breath of God living inside of you.
He is all knowing and reminds you of all that Yeshua said and did.
I AM. The Holy Spirit of God!

The Holy Spirit calls you to reverently fear Adonai.
The Spirit asks you to walk humbly, to be holy and righteous through Yeshua Messiah.
The Spirit empowers you to lift your hands in praise to Yeshua.
He calls you to always love!
I AM. To be Feared!

Yeshua is coming back to earth one day!
Only Adonai knows when Yeshua will return!
He will come down from heaven once again.
It will be incredible!
So keep looking up to the heavens!
He's coming for you!
I AM. Hope!

It is a beautiful mystery of how God is three parts and yet He is ONE!
It is incredibly amazing!
Our Lord God is Supernatural with Divine Powers!
He is Lord over ALL!
I AM. Father, Son, and Holy Spirit!

YOU Are His Everything!

It is important for you to know who Adonai is because He is the one who created you!
He made you for one reason: He loves you!
He knows every detail about you—the color of your eyes and the color of your skin.
He knows the number of hairs on your head.
He knows your personality.
Adonai made you, and you are perfect in Him.
You need to see yourself through the eyes of Adonai, not the eyes of your family, friends, or the world.
Your value comes from Adonai! You are worth far more than all the treasures of this world!
You are the daughter or son of the highest King!
It is when you look at yourself and your unique qualities that the Lord gives you that you can understand your purpose in the Kingdom of God here on earth and in heaven.
You are not made for the world's purpose; you are made for Adonai!
And He has a purpose for you being the way He created you to be!
I AM. The Purpose of your life!

The LORD of this universe wants to have a close relationship with you, inside of your mind and heart.
You are His child, and He created you for fellowship with Him.
The closer you grow to the Lord God, the more you understand who you are.

He wants you to believe in Him and His amazing love for you.
He wants you to be part of His forever family!
Eternal life is a free gift, a present; you just have to accept it.
I AM. Yours!

"For you fashioned my inmost being,
you knit me together in my mother's womb.
I thank you because I am awesomely made,
Wonderfully; your works are wonders –
I know this very well."
Psalm 139:13-14

Adonai's desire is for you to live every day, every minute, every
second, with Him.
His relationship that He wants to have with you is not just for
heaven.
It's for you right now!
His love for you is perfect.
I AM. Waiting!

The Bible says that Adonai loves you so much, but He won't force
you to accept Him as Lord of your life.
If you want to be separated from Adonai, He will grant you that
choice.
He will allow you to die in your sins with the consequences of
hell.
It's your choice, but He wants you so very much!
If pride wells inside of you to rebuke the Lord's authority and
love, please recognize this and humble yourself to Him.
It is a sin for you to be your own god and to live out your own
desires and will.
You are under the authority of the Almighty LORD.
It is so important for you to understand that only Yeshua can
save you.
And it is just as important for you to understand how much He
loves you.

So many who reject Yeshua as the Son of Adonai, and it breaks my heart.

Have they not heard the truth? Do they believe the lies of the enemy?

Yeshua is alive and He is sitting at the right side of His Father, Adonai.

I can't imagine living this life on earth without Yeshua as my source of strength.

He brings me peace and joy! He brings me comfort and healing.

And the thought of anyone being in hell for eternity brings me deep sorrow.

You are now like Eve or you are now like Adam with a freedom to choose.

You have the choice to choose Yeshua as Lord of your life and to break the chains that bind you to death.

I AM. Free Will!

Please don't believe the lies of the enemy.

He whispers lies of hate and destruction.

He whispers lies in your head that you aren't good enough.

Satan is a liar!

He comes to steal your joy and peace.

Guilt and shame are used for deception and to stop you in every area of your life.

The evil one points his nasty finger at you and charges you with things that you have done wrong.

No one is perfect except for Yeshua – that is why He is the only one who could take your place and die for your sins.

I AM. Standing in Your Place!

You must fight His lies with truth!

Adonai tells you that you are loved!

You are forgiven, rescued, and redeemed.

You have been bought with a high price and belong to Him.

Adonai has chosen you, and you are accepted and loved.

You are Adonai's child! You belong to Him!

I AM: For You!

Adonai will tell you that change is needed in your life in order to turn from sin.

He will lovingly walk with you through those changes.

Together, you will make those changes.

He loves you as He teaches you through your choices.

He loves you as you turn to Him and ask for forgiveness.

I AM. Redeemer!

The BATTLE for Your Soul

There is a battle that you cannot see with your eyes.
It is a war for your soul.
And those unseen wars, those spiritual battles, have a physical
and spiritual effect on your world.
Please don't be deceived!
The most critical battles take place *inside* of us – in our minds,
in our emotions, and in our wills.
We can win these battles only when we battle spiritually with
Yeshua.
These battles are manifesting in our physical lives, causing
anguish, pain, and suffering.
These battles against us come from evil spirits.
There are no physical answers to win our spiritual battles.
This is something that I learned when battling for my son.
We have authority through Yeshua to win these battles.
Spiritual battles must be battled with the full armor of God, with
persistent prayer, fasting, and with the Truth that the battles
have already been won by Yeshua.

It is time to prepare for the war!

"Finally, grow powerful in union with the Lord,
in union with His mighty strength!
Use all the armor and weaponry that God provides,
So that you will be able to stand against the deceptive tactics of the
Adversary.
For we are not struggling against human beings,
but against the rulers, authorities and cosmic powers

governing this darkness,
against the spiritual forces of evil
in the heavenly realm.
So take up every piece of war equipment God provides; so that
when the evil day comes, you will be able to resist;
and when the battle is won, you will be standing.
Therefore stand!
Have the belt of truth buckled around your waist,
put on righteousness for a breastplate,
and wear on your feet the readiness that comes from the
Good News of peace.
Always carry the shield of trust, with which you will be able
to extinguish all the flaming arrows of the Evil One.
And take the helmet of deliverance, along with the word given
by the Spirit,
that is, the Word of God;
as you pray at all times, with all kinds of prayers and
requests,
in the Spirit,
vigilantly and persistently,
for all God's people." *Ephesians 6:10-18*

The battles you face are demonic forces that whisper lies in your mind causing hate and destruction,
lies Satan cause you to battle others or even yourself.
And when you dwell on the lies, you give them power over you.
You are no different from Eve in the garden with Satan.
You need to recognize lies of destruction and take authority to demand they leave in the name of Yeshua.
When Satan tempted Yeshua for 40 days in the wilderness,
Yeshua always spoke the words, "It is written." And He fought the battle with scripture.
Yeshua knew that Satan has no power over the Word of Adonai.
For a long time, I would physically put my hand in the air and say out loud, "No, that thought did not come from my Lord. Shut up and go away!"

You don't have to accept thoughts that come into your head. Fight the lies by knowing what the Word of God says as Truth about you!

Fight the lies by praying the Word of God over your life.

Give your thoughts of destruction no power, and ask the Lord to take away any that you may be holding on to.

"For although we do live in the world, we do not wage war in a worldly way; because the weapons we use to wage the war are not worldly. On the contrary, they have God's power for demolishing strongholds. We demolish arguments, and every arrogance that raises itself up against the knowledge of God; we take every thought captive and make it obey the Messiah."
2 Corinthians 10:3-5

As you draw near to Yeshua through His Word and prayer, you will begin to recognize His voice and His words of Truth in your heart.

He does not come to destroy or condemn you – He comes to save, heal, and restore you!

Draw near to Yeshua – He already has won the battle and wants to save you!

Spending time with your Father in prayer, studying and meditating on His word will destroy the enemy's attacks.

The world's court system is very different from the court system of God. In the world's judicial system, when you have a hearing or sentencing, you are found guilty or not guilty. If you are guilty, you are condemned to punishment. The extent of our punishment is linked to the crime. In our Lord's court system, He alone is the only righteous one. We all are guilty of sin. Psalm 51:4 says that *all sin is against God.*

You do have a conviction of guilty. The wonderful, great, amazing truth is that Yeshua stands in your place. He has taken your punishment of sin upon Himself with His own life. He does not mock your sin or laugh at you. He lovingly sets you free! There are no shackles or chains when you decide to live in God's will. The list of sins may be many, but our Lord forgives each and every one of them.

Once you confess your sins to Yeshua, your conviction lasts only as long as you choose to hold on to it in your mind or in your life. When you confess it, and turn from it, it is gone forever. His Word says that He removes your sins and He forgets them! You are free!

"For I will forgive their wickedness and will remember their sins no more."
Jeremiah 31:34

God loves justice, and He loves setting you free!
"For the wages of sin is death,
but the gift of God is eternal life
through Jesus Christ our Lord."
Romans 6:23
Every day I continue to learn about Adonai and His ways.

I can't understand all of Adonai's ways – He is God!

"For My thoughts are not your thoughts,
and your ways are not My ways," says Adonai.
"As high as the sky is above the earth
are my Ways higher than your ways,
and My thoughts than your thoughts."
Isaiah 55:8-9

You can trust Him and trust His love!
You can always count on Him!
Adonai will never, ever fail you!
If you asked Adonai, "Why do you love me?"
He would answer, **"It's simply because you are mine."**
And there's nothing you can do to get the Lord Adonai to love you more than He already does!
He made you, and He's crazy about you!
I AM. Wonderful Counselor!

As you draw close to Him, The Holy Spirit will ask you to Love.
You are called to love Adonai and to love others.
Love is a relationship with Him, and a relationship with others.
As you draw near to Him, your heart will want to love more.
And always remember that Adonai loves you most!
I AM. God of Lovingkindness!

*"He told him, You are to love Adonai your God with all your
heart and with all your soul and with all your strength. This is
the greatest and most important commandment. And a second is
similar to it, You are to love your neighbor as yourself."*
Matthew 23:37-38

Adonai rules over ALL in the heavens and on the earth!
He came down to earth as God
He came down to earth as a human,
And He came down to earth in Spirit, to live inside of you!
Adonai is love!
Adonai the Father, Yeshua the Son, and the Holy Spirit are ONE
God!
He has always been ONE and He will always be ONE!
"I AM THAT I AM" SAYS THE LORD!

PRAYER for Salvation

Maybe you are still questioning what truth really is or who He really is.

My prayer is that the Truth you come to know is the Truth that you come to love and be.

I am asking the Holy Spirit to show you His authority in His Word.

The entire Bible is the living truth of God from beginning to end.

Knowing the Truth is the first step to salvation.

Head knowledge is vital, but it's only the first step to knowing God as your personal Savior.

The Lord longs to go from your knowledge of Him in your head to His presence in your heart and life.

That intimacy only comes by talking to Him alone one on one, just you and Yeshua.

You were born with 5 senses – sight, hearing, smell, taste, and touch.

The people in Yeshua's time were physically able to see God's Son, and yet they still didn't believe.

When you develop the close relationship of talking to Yeshua and listening quietly for His voice, you will know without any doubt that He is who He says He is.

You will sense His presence by trusting.

It's supernatural. It can't be explained.

Trust His truths about Him and His truths about you found in the Word of God.

Your life will be transformed by His presence.

If you want to accept Christ as your Savior and receive everlasting life, I ask you to pray this prayer:
Dear God,
I know I'm a sinner, and I ask for Your forgiveness.
I believe Jesus Christ is Your Son.
I believe that He died for my sins and that You raised Him to life.
I want to trust Him as my Savior and follow Him as my Lord, from this day forward.
Guide my life and help me to do Your will.
I pray this in the name of Jesus. Amen

When you repent and ask the Lord to forgive you of your sin, 1 John 1:19 says:
"For if we confess our sins, He is faithful and just to forgive us our sins and cleanse us from all unrighteousness."
He forgives you!

If you just prayed that prayer, here is what the word of God says:

Joy in Heaven - *"I tell you that in the same way, there will be more joy in heaven over one sinner who turns to God from his sins than over ninety-nine righteous people who have no need to repent."* *Luke 15:7*

Angels Rejoicing - *"In the same way, I tell you, there is joy among God's angels when one sinner repents." Luke 15:10*

JOY - *"Nothing gives me greater joy than hearing that my children are living in the truth." 3 John 1:4*

Please share this great news with someone. Tell someone who also loves Yeshua. They will celebrate with you and will help you begin your close walk with Him. Find a church that loves Yeshua. We are not meant to walk this world alone; we have power unified through Christ.
When you trust in Yeshua Messiah, you are placing your trust in the one who has overcome the world!
He is who He says He is, and you can trust Him.

"Trust in the Lord with ALL your heart, lean not into your own understandings, in all thy ways acknowledge Him and He shall direct your path!"
Proverbs 3:5, 6

Assurance of SALVATION
Salvation through Faith and Trust

Redeemed – *"But Adonai redeems his servants; no one who takes refuge in him will be condemned."*
Psalm 34:22

Trust – *"Yes, indeed! I tell you that whoever hears what I am saying and trusts the One who sent me has eternal life – that is, he will not come up for judgement but has already crossed over from death to life!"*
John 5:24

Eternal Life – *"Whoever trusts in the Son has eternal life. But whoever disobeys the Son will not see that life but remains subject to God's wrath."*
John 3:36

God's Gift – *"For you have been delivered by grace through trusting, and even this is not your accomplishment but God's gift. You were not delivered by your own actions; therefore no one should boast."*
Romans 2:8, 9

Cannot be Snatched – *"And I give them eternal life. They will absolutely never be destroyed, and no one will snatch them from my hands."*
John 10:28

Life in His Son – *"And this is the witness: God has given us eternal life, and this life is in his Son. Those who have the Son have the life, those who do not have the Son of God do not have the life."*
1 John 5:11, 12

"And he said to me, 'It is done!
I am the Alpha
and the Omega,
the Beginning and the End.
To anyone who is thirsty
I myself will give water free of charge
From the Fountain of Life.
He who wins the victory will receive these things,
And I will be his God,
And he will be my son.'"
Revelation 21:6-7

"Our Father in heaven!
May your Name be kept holy.
May your Kingdom come,
Your will be done on earth as in heaven.
Give us the food we need today. [Our daily bread and God's word]
Forgive us what we have done wrong,
as we too have forgiven those who have wronged us.
And do not lead us into hard testing,
But keep us safe from the Evil One.
For kingship, power and glory are Yours forever.
Amen."
Matthew 6:9-13

Heaven Is Going to Be AMAZING!

God will live with His people, and there will no more death, crying, or pain!
"I heard a loud voice from the throne say, 'See! God's divine presence is with mankind, and he will live with them. They will be his people, and he himself, God-with-them, will be their God. He will wipe away every tear from their eyes. There will no longer be any death; and there will no longer be any mourning, crying or pain; because the old order has passed away.'"
Revelation 21:3-4

Out of our imagination – *"No eye has seen, no ear has heard and no one's heart has imagined all the things that God has prepared for those who love him."*
1 Corinthians 2:9

New Heaven and Earth – *"For, look! I create new heavens and a new earth; past things will not be remembered, they will no more come to mind."*
Isaiah 65:17

Heaven's physical appearance – *"It had the Divine presence of God, so that its brilliance was like that of a priceless jewel, like a crystal-clear diamond. It had a great, high wall with twelve gates; at the gates were twelve angels; and inscribed on the gates were the names of the twelve tribes of Israel."*
Revelation 21:11, 12

Night will not exist – *"Night will no longer exist, so they will need neither the light of a lamp nor the light of the sun, because Adonai, God, will shine upon them. And they will reign as kings forever and ever."*
Revelation 22:5

New bodies – *"Furthermore, there are heavenly bodies and earthly bodies; but the beauty of heavenly bodies is one thing, while the beauty of earthly bodies is something else."*
1 Corinthians 15:40

Handicapped healed – *"Then the eyes of the blind will be opened, and the ears of the deaf will be unstopped; the lame man will leap like a deer, and the mute person's tongue will sing."*
Isaiah 35: 5, 6

Animals - Perfect Peace – *"The wolf and the lamb will feed together, and the lion eat straw like an ox."*
Isaiah 65:25

***We will see* Adonai** – *"See what love the Father has lavished on us in letting us be called God's children! For that is what we are. The reason the world does not know us is that it has not known him. Dear friends, we are God's children now; and it has not yet been made clear what we will become. We do not know that when he appears, we will be like him; because we will see him as he really is."*
1 John 3:1, 2

All authority is given to Yeshua in heaven and earth.
"Yeshua came and talked with them. He said, 'All authority in heaven and on earth has been given to me.'"
Matthew 28:18

Army of heaven – *"Therefore, hear the word of Adonai. I saw Adonai sitting on his throne with the whole army of heaven standing on his right and on his left."*
2 Chronicles 18:18

Kingly power rules everything – *"Adonai has established his throne in heaven; his kingly power rules everything. Bless Adonai, you angels of his, you mighty warriors who obey his word, who carry out his orders!"*
Psalm 103:19-21

Houses and vineyards – *"They will build houses and live in them, they will plant vineyards and eat their fruit."*
Isaiah 65:21

Healing of the Nations
"Next the angel showed me the river of the water of life, sparkling like crystal, flowing from the throne of God and of the Lamb. Between the main street and the river was the Tree of Life producing twelve kinds of fruit, a different kind every month; and the leaves of the tree were for healing the nations."
Revelation 22:1, 2

Scriptures of Adonai, Yeshua, and the Holy Spirit – ONE GOD

"As soon as Yeshua had been immersed, he came up out of the water. At that moment heaven was opened, He saw the Spirit of God coming down upon him like a dove,
and a voice from heaven said, 'This is my Son, whom I love; I am well pleased with Him.'"
Matthew 3:16-17

"The angel answered her,
'The Ruach HaKodesh [Holy Spirit] will come over you.
Therefore the holy child born to you
will be called the Son of God.'"
Luke 1:35

"For a child is born to us,
a son is given to us;
dominion will rest on his shoulders,
and he will be given the name
Wonder of a Counselor, Mighty God, Father of Eternity, Prince of Peace."
Isaiah 9:6

"The grace of the Lord Yeshua the Messiah,
the love of God
and the fellowship of the Ruach HaKodesh [Holy Spirit]
be with you all."
2 Corinthians 13:14

"I and the Father are one."
John 10:30

"NOW, 'ADONAI' in this text means the Spirit.
And where the Spirit of ADONAI is, there is freedom."
2 Corinthians 3:17

"My Father, who gave them to me, is greater than all;
and no one can snatch them from the Father's hands.
I and the Father are one."
Once again the Judeans picked up rocks in order to stone him.
Yeshua answered them, "You have seen me do many good deeds
that reflect the Father's power;
For which one of these deeds are you stoning me?"
The Judeans replied, "We are not stoning you for any good deed,
but for blasphemy-
because you, who are only a man, are making yourself out to be
Elohim (God).
Yeshua answered them, "Isn't it written in your Torah, 'I have
said, "You people are Elohim"'?
If he called 'elohim' the people to whom the word of Elohim was
addressed (and the Tanakh cannot be broken), then are you telling
the one whom the Father set apart as holy and sent into the world,
'You are committing blasphemy,' just because I said, 'I am the Son
of Elohim'?
If I am not doing deeds that reflect my Father's power, don't trust
me.
But if I am, then, even if you don't trust me, trust the deeds;
so that you may understand once and for all that the Father is
united with me,
and I am united with the Father."
John 10:29-38

"Let your attitude toward one another be governed by your being
in union with the Messiah Yeshua:
Though he was in the form of God,
He did not regard equality with God

something to be possessed by force.
On the contrary, he emptied himself,
In that He took the form of a slave
by becoming like human beings are.
And when He appeared as a human being,
He humbled himself still more
by becoming obedient even to death—
death on a stake as a criminal!
Therefore God raised Him to the highest place
and gave him the name above every name;
that in honor of the name given Yeshua,
every knee will bow—
in heaven, on earth and under the earth—
and every tongue will acknowledge
that Yeshua the Messiah is Adonai—
to the glory of God the Father.
Philippians 2:5-11

"In the beginning God created the heavens and the earth.
The earth was unformed and void,
Darkness was on the face of the deep,
and the Spirit of God hovered over the surface of the water."
Genesis 1:1-2

"And I will ask The Father, and he will give you another comforting
Counselor like me,
the Spirit of Truth,
to be with you forever.
The world cannot receive him,
because it neither sees nor knows Him.
You know Him, because He is staying with you and will be united
with you."
John 14:16-17

"Moreover, it is God who sets both us and you in firm union with
the Messiah;
he has anointed us,

put his seal on us,
and given us his Spirit in our hearts as a guarantee for the future."
2 Corinthians 1:21-22

"Now there are different kinds of gifts,
but the same Spirit gives them.
Also there are different ways of serving, but it is the same Lord
being served.
And there are different modes of working, but it is the same God
working them all in everyone.
Moreover, to each person is given the particular manifestation of
the Spirit that will be for
the common good."
1 Corinthians 12:4-7

"Yeshua replied to him, "Have I been with you so long without your
knowing me, Philip?
Whoever has seen me has seen the Father;
so how can you say, 'Show us the Father'?
Don't you believe that I am united with the Father; and the Father
united with me?'
What I am telling you, I am not saying on my own initiative;
the Father living in me is doing his own works.
Trust me, that I am united with the Father,
and the Father united me.
But if you can't, then trust because of the works themselves."
John 14:9-11

"For the Kingdom of God is not eating and drinking, but
righteousness, shalom and joy in the Ruach HaKodesh [Holy
Spirit]. Anyone who serves the Messiah in this fashion both pleases
God and wins the approval of other people."
Romans 14:17-18

"From: Kefa, an emissary of Yeshua the Messiah
To: God's chosen people, living as aliens in the Diaspora – in
Pontus, Galatia, Cappadocia, the province of Asia, and Bythinia –

chosen according to the foreknowledge of God the Father
and set apart by the Spirit
for obeying Yeshua the Messiah
and for sprinkling with his blood:
Grace and shalom be yours in full measure."
1 Peter: 1:1-2

"He is the invisible image of the invisible God.
He is supreme over all creation,
because in connection with him were created all things –
in heaven and on earth, visible and invisible,
whether thrones, lordships, rulers or authorities –
they have all been created through him and for him.
He existed before all things,
And he holds everything together."
Colossians 1: 15-17

"Yet for us there is one God, the Father, from whom all things come
and for whom we exist;
and one Lord, Yeshua the Messiah, through whom were created all
things
and through whom we have our being."
1 Corinthians 8:6

"There is one body and one Spirit,
just as when you were called you were called to one hope.
And there is one Lord, one trust, one immersion,
and one God, the Father of all, who rules over all, works through
all and is in all."
Ephesians 4:4-6

"Therefore, go and make people from all nations into talmidin
[disciples],
Immersing them into the reality of The Father, the Son, and the
Ruach HaKodesh [Spirit],
and teaching them to obey everything that I have commanded you.
And remember!

I will be with you always, yes, even until the end of the age."
Matthew 28:19-20

Complete Jewish Bible – An English Version by David H. Stern used for scripture.

CPSIA information can be obtained
at www.ICGtesting.com
Printed in the USA
BVHW030009301020
592148BV00020B/95

9 781950 948352